Co

Task 1
All kinds of plants

These children found different kinds of plants.

What plants grow near your school?

Task 2

Where plants grow

- Make a table like this one.
- Use Task Sheet 1.
  Are there places where no plants grow?
- Why don't plants grow there?

Plants	Where we found them
trees	field
grass	field
pink flowers	flower tub
moss	cracks on the wall
dandelion	field
daisies	field
plantain	cracks in the path
ivy	earth by the fence
bushes	flower bed

Task 3 School plan

Make a plan like this one.

Here is a plan of our school.

We drew pictures of plants.

We stuck our pictures on the plan.

We stuck them in the right places.

Show where you found plants near your school.

Task 4 Be careful

- Tell the story.

- What has happened to the plants?

Task 5

Looking after plants

Here are some gardeners.
They look after their plants.

How do gardeners care for plants?

Task 6 Plant parts

2

- Look at the plants.
  - Find the leaves.
  - Find the flowers.
  - Find the stems.
  - Find the roots.

- Now complete Task Sheet 2

daffodil

foxglove

dandelion

Task 7

Describing plants

Describe a plant.
Use these words to help you.

smooth

shiny

short

thick

tall

thin

trunk

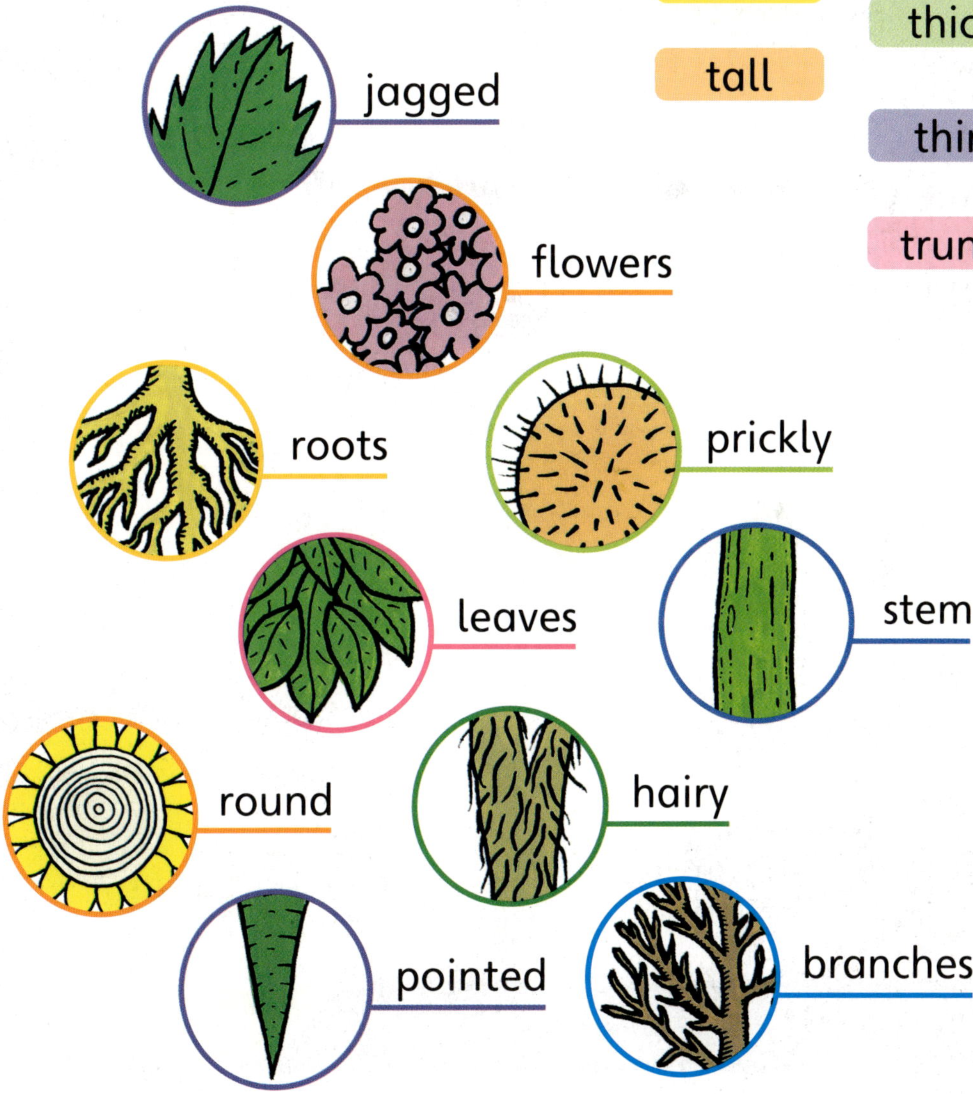

Task 8
Eating plants

- We get lots of food from plants.

  Make a poster like this one.
  Stick on plant pictures

- Which is your favourite food from a plant?

YOU NEED:

Task 9

Growing beans

3

Tom grew a bean plant.
He watched it grow.
He drew pictures and wrote about it.

Plant Diary by Tom

Day 1	Day 4	Day 8
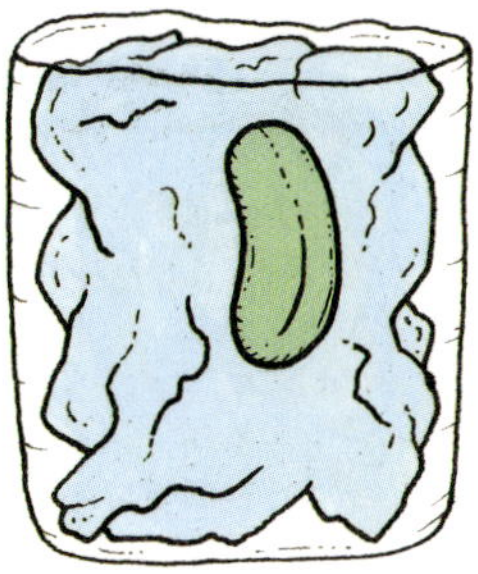	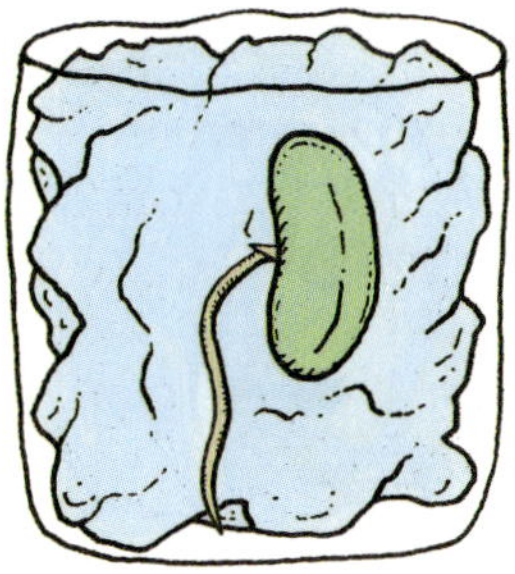	
I planted the seed	It has a root	

Watch your plant grow.
Keep a diary like Tom. Use Task Sheet 3.

Task 10

Do a test

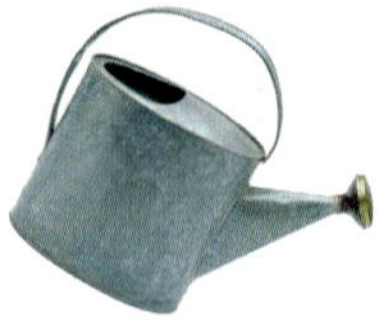

4,5

Some children did a test. They made a table.

- What test were they doing?

How much water	What happened
 Water	
 No water	

- What do you think they put in the empty boxes?

- Do a test like this.

- Make a table. Use Task Sheet 4.

- Now complete Task Sheet 5.

Task 11

Scientific Enquiry

Light test

6

- Do plants need light to grow?
- How could you find out?
- What tests could you do?

- Draw and write about your ideas.
- Do your test.
- Make a table. Use Task Sheet 6.

Task 12

Which is correct?

7

Think about your tests.

Which sentences are correct?

Plants in the dark grow stronger and greener.

Plants die without water.

Plants in the light grow better.

If you give plants water they shrivel up.

Plants need light and water to grow.

Fill in Task Sheet 7.

Task 13

Living plants

8

- Look at some real plants and toy plants.

- Sort them like this.

Living things

Not Living things

- How do you know that a toy plant is not living?

- Complete Task Sheet 8.

poem

I Wonder

I'd really like to know
What you needed to grow
From an acorn so small
To an oak tree this tall.

I wonder if one day
When your acorns fall away,
And sprout roots, leaves and stems,
Will you miss them?

What do you think an acorn needs to grow into a tall oak tree?